BLAZERS

Wild Outdoors

Duck Hunting

by Thomas K. Adamson

Reading Consultant: Barbara J. Fox
Reading Specialist
North Carolina State University

Content Consultant: Greg Slone
Next Generation Hunting
Bowling Green, Kentucky

CAPSTONE PRESS
a capstone imprint

Blazers is published by Capstone Press,
151 Good Counsel Drive, P.O. Box 669, Mankato, Minnesota 56002.
www.capstonepub.com

Books published by Capstone Press are manufactured with paper
containing at least 10 percent post-consumer waste.

Library of Congress Cataloging-in-Publication Data
Adamson, Thomas K., 1970–
Duck hunting / by Thomas K. Adamson.
p. cm.— (Blazers. Wild outdoors)
Includes bibliographical references and index.
Summary: "Describes the equipment, techniques, and safety skills needed for duck
hunting"—Provided by publisher.
ISBN 978-1-4296-4809-7 (library binding)
1. Duck shooting—Juvenile literature. I. Title. II. Series.

SK333.D8A33 2011
799.2'44—dc22   2010001097

Editorial Credits
Christine Peterson, editor; Veronica Correia, designer; Sarah Schuette, photo stylist;
    Marcy Morin, scheduler; Laura Manthe, production specialist

Photo Credits
Capstone Studio/Karon Dubke, all photos except:
Alamy: Daniel Dempster Photography, 22–23, David Wei, 13, Peter Jacobson, 19, Steffan Hill,
    26–27; Shutterstock/Marty Ellis, 7

Artistic Effects
Capstone Press/Karon Dubke (woods); Shutterstock: rvika (wood), rvrspb (fence), VikaSuh (sign)

Printed in the United States of America in Stevens Point, Wisconsin.
102010
005977R

Table of Contents

Chapter 1

Take Aim!

You and a friend wait patiently in the brush near open water. A group of mallard ducks flies low across the sky. They fly toward your location, but you don't fire.

Wild Fact:

Puddle ducks include the black duck, mallard, pintail, and wood duck. Puddle ducks are found in rivers and ponds.

Wild Fact:

Diving ducks include the scamp, canvasback, redhead, goldeneye, and bufflehead. These ducks dive underwater to get food.

The ducks circle around and fly closer to your spot. You both take aim and fire. Two ducks drop into the water. Success!

mallard

Chapter 2

Getting Ready

Hunters bring down ducks with shotguns. These guns fire shells filled with small beads called **shot**. Shotguns are best at close **range**. With shotguns, hunters can hit ducks less than 50 yards (46 meters) away.

shot—lead or steel pellets that can be fired from a shotgun
range—the greatest distance ammunition can travel to reach its target

Wild Fact:

Shot travels more than 1,200 feet
(366 meters) per second.

shell

Duck hunters dress for cold, wet weather. They wear warm clothes and dress in layers. **Camouflage** clothing helps hunters hide from ducks. Hunters also wear rubber hip boots or chest **waders**.

camouflage—coloring that makes hunters blend in with their surroundings

waders—long waterproof boots used for fishing or duck hunting

waders

Hunters use **blinds** to stay hidden from ducks. Hunters cover blinds with grass, leaves, or tall weeds. Some hunters buy blinds that are covered with camouflage.

camouflage blind

blind— a hidden place from which hunters can shoot prey

Wild Fact:

Hunting dogs are trained to get used to the sound of gunfire.

Hunting dogs **retrieve** fallen ducks for hunters. The dogs sit quietly in the blind. They wait for a hunter's command before getting a duck. They carry birds without damaging them.

retrieve—to get or bring something back

Duck Hunting Equipment

decoys

face mask

camouflage
clothing

duck
blind

boots

binoculars

waders

shotgun

shells

calls

hunting
license

17

Chapter 3

Skills and Techniques

Hunters use **decoys** to attract ducks. The plastic or wooden decoys look like real ducks. Hunters place decoys near their blinds. They spread out the decoys so ducks have room to land.

decoy—a model of a duck used to attract real ducks

decoys

Some decoys look like
ducks sleeping or eating.

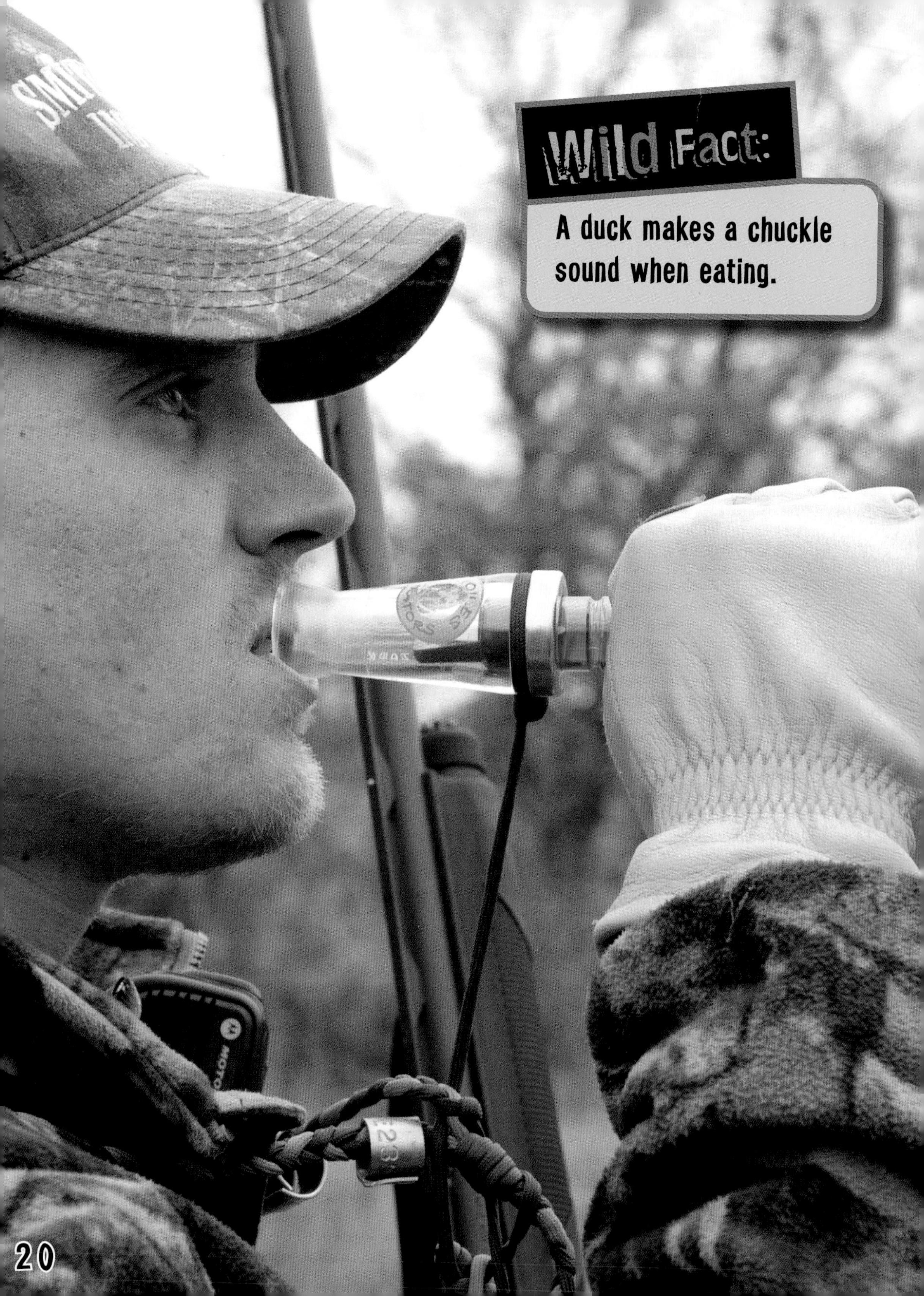

Wild Fact:

A duck makes a chuckle sound when eating.

Hunters fool ducks by using **calls**. Ducks make different sounds when eating and mating. Hunters copy these sounds with duck calls. Hunters practice calls to get the right sounds.

Shooting a duck in flight takes skill and practice. Hunters follow the duck with their gun **barrels**. They swing their guns forward and aim just ahead of the duck.

barrel—the long, tube-shaped metal part of a gun through which bullets or pellets travel

Wild Fact:

Hunters of both ducks and geese are called waterfowlers.

Chapter 4

Be Safe

For duck hunters, nothing is more important than using guns safely. Hunters never point guns at other people. Hunters keep the gun **safety** on until they are ready to shoot.

shotguns

safety—a device that prevents a gun from firing

Wild Fact:

Hunters keep their guns unloaded until they are out hunting. They unload their guns when they are done hunting.

Hunters practice their shooting skills year-round. They shoot clay disks that are launched into the air. Hunters can bring down more birds with practice.

Wild Fact:

In addition to hunting licenses, duck hunters buy federal duck stamps. Money from stamps is used to save duck habitats.

Chapter 5

Bag Some Ducks!

Think you can outsmart a duck? You have to start early in the morning. You may have to brave the cold, wet weather. But the thrill of bagging some ducks can't be beat!

Glossary

barrel (BAYR-uhl)—the long, tube-shaped metal part of a gun through which bullets or pellets travel

blind (BLYND)—a hidden place from which hunters can shoot prey

call (KAWL)—a device that makes sounds like a duck

camouflage (KA-muh-flahzh)—coloring that makes hunters blend in with their surroundings

decoy (DEE-koy)—a model of a duck used to attract real ducks

range (RAYNJ)—the greatest distance ammunition can travel to reach its target

retrieve (ri-TREEV)—to get or bring something back

safety (SAYF-tee)—a device that prevents a gun from firing

shot (SHOT)—lead or steel pellets that can be fired from a shotgun

waders (WAY-durz)—long waterproof boots used for fishing or duck hunting

Read More

Frahm, Randy. *Duck Hunting.* The Great Outdoors. Mankato, Minn.: Capstone Press, 2008.

Lewis, Joan. *Hunting.* Get Going! Hobbies. Chicago: Heinemann Library, 2006.

Wilson, Jef. *Hunting for Fun!* For Fun! Minneapolis: Compass Point Books, 2006.

Internet Sites

FactHound offers a safe, fun way to find Internet sites related to this book. All of the sites on FactHound have been researched by our staff.

Here's all you do:

Visit *www.facthound.com*

Type in this code: **9781429648097**

Index